Early Farm Life

Lise Gunby

The Early Settler Life Series

Toronto
New York

Crabtree Publishing Company

To my grandparents

*A special thanks to the following people without
whose help this book would not have been possible:*

Editor-in-chief: *Bobbie Kalman*
Editor: *Susan Hughes*
Assistant editors: *Carla Williams*
 Mary Ann Horgan
 Maria Protz
Freelance editor: *Dan Liebman*
Design and mechanicals: *Nancy Cook*
 Diane Taylor
Photographers: *Sarah Peters*
 Stephen Mangione
 Donna Acheson
Librarians: *Margaret Crawford Maloney*
 Dana Tenny
 Jill Shefrin
 Stanley Triggs
 Peder Bjerre

*A thank you to Arnie Krause for keeping us
on schedule*

Cataloging in Publication Data

Gunby, Lise, 1959 -
 Early Farm Life

(Early settler life series)
Includes index.
ISBN 0-86505-027-9 hardcover
ISBN 0-86505-026-0 softcover

1. Agriculture - History. 2. Farm life - History.
I. Title. II. Series.

S437.G86 1983 630'.9'03

*102 Torbrick Avenue
Toronto M4J 4Z5*

*350 Fifth Avenue
Suite 3308
New York, N.Y. 10001*

Contents

This farm land is still a forest! These settlers have built a log cabin for their shelter and a roof on stilts to protect their small harvest. The settler hauls logs. He is going to build a shanty for his oxen. It is hard to believe that these trees will all be chopped down to make way for fields.

Destination: Wilderness

Many settlers who came to the New World to farm had never even lived in the country. They arrived at their land with everything they possessed packed in a wagon. They looked around and saw that their farm was just a forest! They owned nothing but trees, a few pots and pans, some flour, a couple of hens, a milk cow, and the two oxen pulling their wagon. There was nothing else to do in the wilderness except take heart and get to work!

One of the first important jobs was finding a river or spring for water. Dinner was hard cakes made of flour and water cooked in a frying pan over an open fire. The family could hunt for wild animals and wild fruit to eat. The children broke off leafy branches for the milk cow because there was so little grass.

Building a home

The first shelter was made of logs. Trees were important because farmers needed the wood to build their houses, barns, fences, furniture, and tools. As the trees were chopped down, the buildings and fences were built up. The animals had to make do outdoors because there was no time to build a barn. The family was busy planting their first crop so they would not starve.

A few families had enough money to buy cleared land. The settlers who had cleared the land earned some money by selling their farm. They moved deeper into the woods to clear more land.

4

These settlers have just finished building a new house with windows. Their first home was the log shanty. They will use the old shanty to store crops and shelter animals. They have been hard at work chopping trees. You can see the stumps, and the settlers can see the light from their new windows!

This picture shows what people mean by "roughing it in the bush." This settler is doing his laundry in a wheelbarrow! He had to boil water in a pail over an open fire. He does not have any soap, but he does not mind scrubbing. His clothes get filthy when he works in the bush.

Westward bound

Perils on the prairie

Farmers across the country experienced many sorrows. Bad weather could destroy a whole season's worth of work. The death of an ox could make it impossible for the farmer to get his crop in. Wild animals helped themselves to the crops.

Prairie farmers had special problems. The locust plague was one of the nastiest tricks nature played on the prairie farmer. Nothing made the farmer feel more helpless.

The locusts eat everything!

The weather on the prairie grew very hot and dry. Locusts, or large grasshoppers, would hatch in unusually large numbers. Once locusts started to multiply, nothing could stop these nasty green pests from eating every plant in sight. Even the trees would be completely covered with locusts. They crunched everything in their path. The noise continued for days as the locusts ate and ate. The sound was so hard on the farmers' nerves that some of them almost went mad listening to it! It was horrible even to step outside the house because in a minute farmers were covered with the big, creepy insects.

The pests disappear

Finally the day came when there was nothing left for the locusts to eat. As quickly as they had come, they took to the sky and flew away!

Imagine the grief of the farm family as they looked out over the fields that they had planted so carefully. They comforted one another and set to work once more.

The lonely land

The prairie was a lonely place. Settlers complained that the flat land, which seemed to go on forever without a hill or tree, was ugly. The space and the loneliness of the prairie were heartbreaking. Sometimes the prairie made you feel as if there were no other human beings in the world.

Finally the settlers began to feel at home on the prairie. They grew to love the endless flat land. They worked hard and were rewarded with fields of golden wheat that seemed as wide as the sea. To the prairie settlers, nothing could be more beautiful than the sight of wheat waving in the wind.

The locust

These prairie settlers certainly look glum. All they have to show for months of hard work is a big pile of buffalo bones! They are sick of buffalo steak. They are waiting to harvest their wheat crop. Their house is built of squares of sod cut from the earth. It looks lumpy, but it is home!

This family is trying to stop the locusts from multiplying and eating the rest of their crops. They are burning the locusts and the crop that the insects have attacked. The children are happy to help sweep these horrible grasshoppers into the pile.

Father is up with the sun and out into the bush every morning. All day long he chops at the stubborn old trees. The sounds of chopping and crashing never seem to stop. Mary is up early, too. She is collecting kindling for the kitchen fire.

Believe it or not, this crossroads grew up and became a busy town. The painter finally got some customers! The land was not a pretty sight just after it had been cleared. The trees have been chopped down and burned. There are scorched stumps everywhere.

The fall of the giants

The most important tool the new farmer owned was a strong, sharp ax. By the time the settlers cleared enough land to sow crops, they could not stop their arms from swinging! Every long, hard day the forest echoed with the sound of chopping. Tree after tree came crashing down. On one settler's farm, the cows learned to follow the chopper into the woods. They knew that the fallen trees had delicious leaves.

When the settlers arrived in the spring, they cleared enough land to grow a small crop for the family to eat during the winter. When a family arrived in the fall, they marked off the land to be cleared that winter by notching the trees at the corners of their property. Every frosty morning the farmer would be out chopping trees. He must have felt as if the trees had grown up again overnight.

There were different ways of clearing away the huge old trees to make way for crops. The first job was chopping and clearing the small trees and bushes with a small ax or tool called a **bushwhack**. The under-brush was piled and burned.

When the ground was cool enough to work on again, the farmer could chop the big trees. A common way was to fell the trees and leave them until they dried. Then they were rolled into a pile and burned.

Some settlers did not do the hard work of chopping the trees. Instead they **girdled** the trees by cutting a circle in the bark around the trunks. The trees starved to death without the food and water that travels up through the bark. This method was dangerous, because as the tree branches died, they fell off and often hurt people and animals. Before they fell, the girdled tree trunks shaded the land, and the crops planted around them could not get enough sun.

The eager settlers who needed to plant fields in the first season of their farm life could not wait for the trees to dry or die. **Wind-row felling** was a quick way to make room for a crop. The trees were chopped so that they fell in rows. One line of trees was pushed to the right, and another line was pushed to the left. The trees fell on top of one another in rows, and were burned in the field.

9

Settlers learned the importance of cooperation. Neighbors helped one another at logging bees. The workers brought their teams of oxen to haul the logs into a pile so they could be burned. Logging was a hard job, but working with friends made it easier.

Fire! The settlers are burning the stubborn stumps. They had to be careful that the fire did not burn out of control.

Blast those trees!

Many settlers described the burning of the trees. One settler admired the burning pine trees which sent off "showers of sparks that whirled about like rockets and fire-wheels in the wind." Some farmers held a logging bee. Neighbors came with their teams of oxen and helped to cut down and pile the trees. The workers finished as night fell. The piles were set on fire. "On a dark night," wrote one settler, "a hundred or two hundred of these large heaps all on fire at once are a fine sight. They shed a broad glare of light for a great distance. During the month of July in the new settlements, the whole country is lit up by these fires at night."

The settlers cleared only as much land as they were able to plant. They knew that the trees would sprout up again if the land was not used for crops. The farm family cleared a little more land each year.

Potash

The ashes from the burned trees were raked into piles and saved to make lye. Water trickling through the ashes turned into lye. Lye was used to make soap. The water in the lye was boiled away in a pot and this solid lye was called potash. So much potash was made when the New World was cleared that it was sold to Europe.

After the logs were burned, the farmer was still left with the stumps. The stumps were stubborn and hard to burn. Most farmers left the stumps in the ground to rot. Later, they could be pulled out. A chain was attached to the oxen. The chain was wrapped around the stump. The oxen pulled in a circle around the stump and twisted the root out of the ground. Some determined farmers dug out the stumps. Others were delighted to blast them out with gunpowder.

Choppers and loggers

In the early days of settlement, some settlers became experts at clearing land. New settlers paid them to chop down the underbrush and trees on their farm. These "choppers" knew how important their axes were. One chopper kept his ax under his pillow so that it would always be shiny and sharp. Can you see how this might be a dangerous way to keep an ax safe?

Some farmers also worked as loggers. They spent the winters in the bush. In the warm seasons they raised crops and animals, selling the food they produced to the loggers who did not have farms. Almost everyone could be called a farmer. Doctors, millers, ministers, blacksmiths, and other townspeople kept cows for milk, pigs for meat, and hens for eggs.

"I'll pull this stump if it's the last thing I do!" Clearing land was backbreaking work, but there was no time to complain.

*These farmers work in the bush as loggers when they are not working on their farms. One man is sharpening his ax on a **grindstone**.*

11

These farmers have saved the biggest stone for last. First they had to dig around the rock so they could attach the chain. That part of the operation was bad enough. Even the oxen are finding this a heavy load. Willy cracks the whip and shouts encouragement.

"Why not save our strength?" These men are on their way to pick stones from the fields. Two of them are hitching a ride in the stoneboat. The ox will wait patiently until the stoneboat is filled. Then he will pull the load into the center of the field where the farmers pile the stones.

Stumps and stones make beautiful fences which last for years. The roots of the pine trees are thick and gnarled. Nature knows how to make beautiful designs.

Stumps and stones...

Logs and stumps were not the only nuisances the farmer had to worry about. Stones had to be picked by hand. Oxen helped to haul the big stones and rocks. Some farmers had a wagon called a **stoneboat** to carry away the rocks. Many farmers unloaded the rocks in the middle of their fields. On some farms today you can still see the old stone piles.

Fencing the farm

Stumps and stones made good fences. Stones picked from the fields were simply piled around the edges of the fields. The stumps of pine trees made fences that lasted many years because the pitch in the wood preserved it. The straightest logs were cut into even lengths and then split into quarters called **rails.** The best kinds of wood for rail fences were cedar, oak, ash, and chestnut. They split cleanly and never seemed to wear out. Rail fences were built about eight rails high. They were called "snake" or "worm" fences because they formed a zigzag pattern. Have you ever seen these fences in the country?

A neatly fenced farm was beautiful. Good fences made good neighbors. A farmer's animals did not invite themselves to dinner in the neighbor's fields!

The rails are stacked at an angle to make a fence. When the fence is finished, it will have a zigzag pattern.

13

The cabin was built from the trees that once grew where the cabin now stands. The family hopes to chop enough logs to build a small barn before winter comes. They also hope they can have glass in the cabin windows. Now they use greased paper. It lets the light in, but you get a foggy view!

Father holds the tree branch down so Matthew can aim accurately. There are so many deer on their farm that the family never runs out of meat. The deer often come to this spot for water. Deer cannot see very well but they have a keen sense of smell. Father and Matthew must be downwind.

Mary's letter to Grandmother

Mary came to the backwoods with her parents, brothers, and sister. Her new life was hard. She learned quickly to be brave and cheerful. In this letter to her grandmother Mary describes her family's experiences.

Dear Grandmother,

The mail is so slow here and the cost of mailing a letter is so dear that I am afraid you will hear little from us. We think of you often and trust you are well. Father, Mother, Matthew, John, Beth, and I thought it would be cheerful to spend one evening at rest and leave the work for a short time. What could be more cheerful than writing to you! Father must carry the grain to the mill tomorrow and promises to arrange delivery of our letter. It is our first crop of wheat and we are quite proud of it even though it fills only a single sack.

We are gathered around our table. It is not exactly a kitchen table because our cabin has only one room. Our table is special. You will be surprised to hear that it is built on a stump, and that we built our cabin around the stump just so we could put our table top upon it! Our little log home is certainly cosy but we long for floors made of wood rather than dirt.

Our first home was a wigwam!

I am getting ahead of myself and must begin at the beginning. Our first home was even cosier. You would never guess, but it was a wigwam! Mr. Percy, who guided us to our property, helped us to build the wigwam so we would have shelter during our first night. We cut down young trees with forked ends and made a cone shape by leaning the poles against one another at their tops. Then we covered our frame with branches. We felt quite safe and snug, and soon had a fire crackling away outside the door of the wigwam. We kneaded together flour and water to make flat little cakes to toast. We were so hungry that we thought them delicious! My friends in the old country would never believe our adventures. Our life is like something from a book. I can hardly believe it myself!

On our first morning Father shot a deer and we had meat and flour cakes. It is strange to be able to hunt our dinner from our very doorstep. Altogether this is a strange country. One day we freeze, and the next day we boil.

We eat funny food!

I shall not tire you with descriptions of all our meals, but I must tell you of some of the odd things we eat. We make coffee with acorns and dandelion roots. We even manage to swallow tea made from the bread we burn by mistake. Nothing is wasted. Mother is thankful that there are so many rabbits, pigeons, and wild turkeys that they almost jump into her cooking pot. The pigeons are so plentiful that they cover the ground like a thick blanket. There is so much of some kinds of food, and so little of other kinds! Father spent a day chopping trees, and when we awoke the next morning there was a fat turkey sitting on almost every stump. The babies, Beth and John, are a little ill from eating so much meat. They are also just plain sick of it!

It was a hard blow when our potato crop rotted because of wet weather. Of course, there was not much left of the potatoes, turnips, cabbages, or corn by the time the squirrels, grasshoppers, raccoons, and rabbits had their meals. Mother sends Beth, John, and me out to the field with pots and pans to frighten away the pests. We cannot always be banging and playing at being scarecrows, however. The little squirrels, you know, can scoop out a potato and leave the skin, neat as you please! I have seen them carry off a cob of corn longer than they are. I would like squirrels if they did not steal the food from our mouths. I am afraid the squirrels are severely punished, however. They eat our food, and we eat them!

Matthew earns our bread

Matthew has been helping Father with the chopping, but he plans to make tools for the neighbors. They will pay him with food, which, if you ask my stomach, is worth more than money! He has already made us a wagon, chairs, water buckets, barrels, a spinning wheel, and a yoke for the oxen!

15

I learn my lessons the hard way

Dear Grandmother, I try to work as hard as Matthew and to be a good girl but it is a hard task. The mosquitoes are almost as big as the squirrels. We have been picking berries for days so we will have preserves for the winter. I shall never stop shivering at the howls of the wolves. Father tells me not to be silly because wolves are just wild dogs. He says that the howl of a wolf is worse than his bite. The howl, Grandmother, is bad enough. There are many awful stories about wolves, but I shall not frighten you by telling them. Instead I shall make you smile by telling you of our new pet. Ebony is a black fox. His mother was killed in a trap and our mother cat has adopted him.

Mother hurt her leg

Our clothes are beginning to look like rags. We have no well and must carry water from the river. Poor Father had sunstroke last month and Mother went out to chop trees. The ax slipped and put a great gash in her leg. She is healing quickly now, but it was hard for me to keep my head when I followed the sound of her cries and found her bleeding in the bush. We had to sell our horse to buy another cow when dear old Bessie died. Our neighbors live so far away that we do not see them except when there is work to be done. I do believe that Father, who is so good and cheerful, will be too tired to smile when he returns from the mill.

He must walk for days to get to the mill and back. Then he must help the Andersons raise their barn. We have not built our barn yet, but Father hopes to put up a shanty before the snow falls so that our new milk cow will live through the winter cold.

Please excuse my complaints

Please excuse the brown writing paper and my complaints. We all have great hopes for the future. I am learning many new skills, although I am learning the hard way. Yesterday I heard the call of a wild turkey gobbler. I told Father, who went out with his rifle and came back with our dinner.

The beaver meadow

Last week John and I were out exploring. We were walking through a dark, thick wood. We suddenly came upon a beautiful meadow, as green and shining as an emerald in the sun! It was a beaver meadow. The beavers had made a dam in the stream nearby and this had formed a pond. The pond formed by the dam flooded the forest, and all the trees in the pond died. When the beavers moved on, the dam broke up, and the land that was covered by water was drained, leaving this meadow. The sight of the beaver meadow took our breath away. Father says it will grow excellent hay.

Mother asks if it is possible for you to send some garden seeds, especially peas. She says we shall all be wonderfully fat after the next harvest. It is hard to think of waiting that long. Everyone sends love.

Your granddaughter, Mary

◄ Mary writes to her grandmother that there are so many pigeons that they cover the ground like a blanket. Many settlers told similar stories about these **passenger pigeons**. One settler described tree branches breaking off trees because so many pigeons were sitting on them.

Passenger pigeons became scarce because they were hunted so frequently. Today they are extinct. Other animals also suffered when people tamed the wilderness. Deer are hard to find today. Wild turkeys are also rare. Settlers probably would not have believed that the supply of these animals could run out.

Have you ever seen a beaver dam? These dams are sophisticated! Even engineers are impressed by them. Busy beavers could finish a dam and move in faster than the settlers could build their cabins. Of course, beavers had sharp front teeth to work with.

This berry patch is too big! For days the family has been picking and eating, picking and eating. They are getting tired of wild fruit. "Let's bury the berries," suggests John. A sense of humor helps. They depend on wild crops because they have not yet grown their own food.

17

Grandfather saves the best ears of Indian corn. He shells the kernels from the cob. He will plant the kernels next spring. Grandfather has the best corn in the community. For many seasons he has been hand-picking his crop.

18

This is a big day for Paddy, Colleen, and Sean. They are harvesting the first potato crop on their farm. The family came from Ireland where the potato crop often would fail to grow. Now they have potatoes to last all winter. They will even share them with the animals in the barn.

The first season on the farm

The settlers had to plant their first crops around the stumps dotting their new fields. They planted vegetables for the family to eat. They prayed for a good first harvest to save them from going hungry. They often planted vegetable seeds in little hills of earth. They also dug holes with an ax or a hoe to plant potatoes, turnips, squash, pumpkins, and Indian corn. The settlers planted pumpkins and squash between the rows of corn. They learned this efficient method of planting from the Indians. In this way, two useful crops could be planted in one small clearing. The wide leaves of the pumpkin plant grew close to the ground and prevented the soil from drying out.

The Indian corn crop

The settlers used Indian corn to make porridge, pudding, and cornmeal for bread and cakes. The kernel was ground with a mortar and pestle made from hard wood. The coarse pieces were cooked and served as a vegetable called **hominy.** The settlers used all of the corn plant. "Waste not, want not," was

an important motto for the farm family. The pigs enjoyed the husks removed from the heads of corn. The husks were used to stuff mattresses or were woven into collars for the horses and mats for the house. When the kernels were removed from the cob, the cob could be used to make corks for bottles. Meat smoked over a corncob fire had a delicious flavor. When the cobs burned into ashes, the ashes were used like baking powder for raising cakes.

The family shared their garden crops with their pigs, cows, and chickens. Other animals helped themselves. The settlers had to guard their crops from the raids of chipmunks, blue-jays, raccoons, bears, and many other hungry birds and animals of the forest.

19

Working up a wheat field

When enough land was cleared, farmers planted wheat. The settlers could not turn the land with a plow because there were too many stumps blocking the field. They used **harrows** to stir up the soil.

Many harrows were built in the shape of a triangle and had teeth made of wood or iron which raked the soil. The triangular shape could be pulled between the tree stumps more easily than a square or rectangular shape. The earliest harrows were just heavy branches or tree tops which scraped the earth. The settlers called the harrow a

"butterfly" or a "wild goose" because it bounced wildly over the bumpy new field.

Harrows could be pulled by the farmer who did not have an ox or a horse to pull a plow. Even when the farmer had patient oxen to pull the harrow, the job was frustrating. The harrow caught on stumps and stones.

The farmer harrowed a new field three or four times to break up the earth. The grain was sown by **broadcasting.** The farmer walked back and forth over the field scattering the seed by hand. Then he harrowed the land again so that the seed was lightly covered with earth.

On early farms, oxen were more common than horses. Oxen were steady, patient, and strong. They did not get excited when the plow was caught on a rock or root. They kept plugging. They were slow, but they were sure!

The farmer looked forward to the day when he could buy a team of horses. Oxen were dependable but they were not very fast. Plow horses worked in the fields, and they could also be hitched to the wagon when the farmers wanted to go to town.

Jean, Mother, and Flora have been out for a walk. They are delighted by the improvements on their farm. The original barn is now a chicken coop. There is a machinery shed, a dairy, and a stable for the horses. The cattle graze happily around the stumps that still sit in the meadow.

It is high noon and everyone stops working to enjoy a picnic for dinner. Harvesting hay was a family affair.

From poverty to plenty

As the first hard year became a memory, the farm family could be proud of their strength and courage. The rough clearing in the bush began to look like a farm with neatly fenced fields and fat, contented live-stock. A large crop of wheat was sprouting where the potatoes, corn, and pumpkins had been planted the first season. More land was being cleared. The farmer was planning to sow the older clearings with oats, rye, buckwheat, and hay. He planted different crops each year so that the soil would not be worn out. This is called "crop rotation." Tired soil sprouts weeds instead of healthy plants. In a few years the last of the stumps could be pulled and the farmer could make or buy a plow to dig deeply into the rich soil. The same family that had complained because they had nothing to eat but bread and turnips, now complained because their crop was so good they could not manage to harvest it all by themselves.

The old gray mare has pulled the wagon to a stop in front of the barn. Now it is time to fork the hay into the **mow.** Even the smallest children could be helpful at haying time.

Davey is trying out the new corn reaper. It works! The machine cuts the stalks and dumps them into neat piles. Davey can't believe he is sitting down on the job!

These workers have a long way to go. How will all these pieces fit together? Luckily, these men are experts. They have helped many neighbors build barns.

The barn is up, and everyone is working quickly to make sure it stays that way. The poles at the bottom are propping up the beams. The men on the frame are making sure that it is secure.

This barn looks so good that the family might be tempted to move in. The animals can have the house! Barns were often beautiful works of architecture. Notice the lightning rods on the roof and the ramp to the threshing floor.

A home for the animals

First the settlers built themselves a home. Then they tried to find time to build a small log shanty for the animals before the arrival of winter. Often the animals had to be left outside in the cold until the settlers could erect a barn.

The farmer builds a barn

After the land was cleared and after a sawmill was built in a community nearby, farmers were able to build frame barns. They held barn-raising bees to help one another provide shelter for animals and crops. Barn raising was dangerous. After a foundation of wooden blocks was laid, the pieces of the frame, called "bents," were raised with long poles. Rafters to support the roof of the barn were attached to the top of the bents. Workers swarmed over the frame like ants. Somehow they made it through the barn raising without tumbling to the ground.

There were styles of barns for different tastes and needs. Some barns were built in the shape of an L. Others were U-shaped with a courtyard in the middle. Many barns were built into a hill so that part of the dairy and stable was underground. Stables nestled into a hill were warm in the winter and cool in the summer. The farmer could drive wagons up a ramp to the top floor of the barn where the crops were stored. The upper floor contained the granary, hay and straw mows, a place for tool storage, and a threshing floor.

A crib for the corn

Many farms had a corn crib made of slats of wood. The slats had to be spaced wide enough so that air could keep the corn dry, and close enough that animals could not steal the crop. The corn crib was built on stilts in an open area so that the air and wind could dry the corn. Wet corn soon grew moldy. Settlers often turned pails over the tops of the stilts before they put the crib on top so that rats and mice could not scurry up the legs and into the corn.

25

Sky signals

The early farmers were able to read the sign language of nature. They had to know when to plant crops and how to protect them. An entire crop could be destroyed by dry weather, too much rain, or frost. Here is one farmer's system of weather forecasting. According to this farmer, certain dew, sky, cloud, and wind signs indicated what weather to expect in the near future. Try this system and decide for yourself. Do you find this an accurate way to judge the changes in the weather?

What you see → → → → → → → → → → *What you get*

Dew signs
- *a heavy dew after a fair day*
- *a light dew and no wind*

  ▶ *another fair day*
  ▶ *rain*

Sky signs
- *a red sky as the sun sets*
- *a red sky in the morning*
- *a sea-green sky during rain*
- *a deep blue sky during rain*

  ▶ *fine weather*
  ▶ *bad weather*
  ▶ *rain will increase*
  ▶ *showers*

Cloud signs
- *clouds growing bigger very quickly*
- *clouds that look like horses' tails*
- *a bright sky and clouds like the fleece of sheep, but with dark centers*
- *high, thin clouds like a trail of wool*
- *a cloud-covered sky with small black clouds flying underneath the top layer*
- *a fog on hilltops*
- *a fog on fields*
- *an evening rainbow*

  ▶ *thunder*
  ▶ *wind*
  ▶ *hail, snow, or rain*

  ▶ *wind and a good chance of rain*
  ▶ *a long rain*

  ▶ *rain*
  ▶ *sun*
  ▶ *strong wind*

Wind signs
- *an east wind*
- *a wind that changes direction slowly*
- *a wind that changes direction quickly*

  ▶ *bad weather*
  ▶ *fair weather*
  ▶ *bad weather with wind storms*

Moonshine

The Moon and the weather
May change together,
But the change of the Moon
Does not change the weather.
If we had no Moon at all,
And that may seem strange,
We still would have weather
That is subject to change.

The farmer's welfare depends on the weather.

The children add their weight to the snowplow. They are pretending to be arctic explorers. Joyce is so cold that she is tired of the game. She tries to think about spring. Father is proud of his new invention. He made the snowplow by nailing boards in the shape of a triangle.

Frozen up and snowed in

Winter was the season that everybody loved to hate. The settlers did indeed have good reason to detest the cold. Settlers had memories of winters in the backwoods that froze in their minds for a lifetime. Here a settler remembers a winter morning in the log cabin of his childhood.

"It was grand to sit at night before the roaring mountain of fire and forget the cold outside, but it was a frightful thing to dress in the morning in the bitter cold of the bedrooms. The windows were thick with frost and the water was frozen solid at my side. If I wet my hairbrush the water on the bristles would often freeze in a moment. Water in my wash basin sometimes froze around the edges as I was washing.

"The tears would come out of our eyes and freeze on our cheeks as they rolled down. The towels were regularly frozen like a board if they had been at all damp. Water brought in overnight in buckets and put

as close to the fire as possible had to be broken with an ax in the morning.

"Loaves of bread were as hard as stones. They sparkled because of the ice in them. The milk froze on the way from the barn to the house, and even while we were milking. We were happy if we could thaw our meat long enough to cook it!"

Settlers could not afford the luxury of huddling by the fire. The family trudged bravely through the drifts to the barn to see to the animals, even though it was possible to wander off the path from the house to the barn and freeze to death.

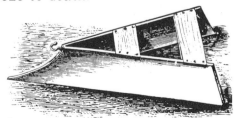

A snowplow

27

Winter work

Even in the winter the farmer had enough to do that he could always work up a sweat to keep warm. Here is a list of questions a farmer could ask himself in February.

Have you:

- cut your wood and piled it up for next summer?
- examined your bees?
- got your spouts ready for tapping the trees and your buckets ready for making sugar?
- drawn your logs to the sawmill?
- racked off your cider and mended your cider casks?
- put your hams in the smokehouse?
- threshed out all of your grain?
- sorted your potatoes in the cellar?
- felled and split your trees for rails?
- collected your **cions** for grafting in the spring?
- repaired your harrows, plows, carts, yokes, hoes, forks, and harness?
- taken a load of wood to the poor?

If you have done all these things, you have done well.

Sap from the maple trees is taken to the center of the bush where the settlers build a fire. They boil the water off the sweet sap to make maple syrup.

The sap flows in the early spring

Making maple syrup was a joyful event. Winter was over and spring had sprung. The best sap flowed from the south side of the maple trees early in the spring. The sap ran best when the days were sunny and the nights were frosty. Later in the maple-syrup season, the best sap came from the north side of the trees.

The settlers drilled a spout into the trunks of the trees. The sap flowed through the spout into a pail or trough. The settlers carried the sap into the center of the sugar bush. Settlers with many maple trees sometimes carried the sap in barrels on a sleigh pulled by an ox or a strong worker.

Turning sap into sugar

The sap was boiled in big kettles. Often milk, the fat from pork, or eggs were added to the sap in order to make it clear. The best **clarifier** was eggs. The sap was boiled and the eggs rose to the top along with any dirt that was in the sap. The eggs and dirt were skimmed from the syrup and it was boiled again. The syrup was just right if it hardened at once when it was thrown on the snow. One of the best parts of maple-syrup making was testing the syrup. The syrup could be boiled until it was so thick that it could be used in the place of sugar.

The blossoming of spring

The spring season was full of joy. Winter was forgotten as the world of nature bloomed. The farmers are busy planting crops, but Grandfather and Stephen take the time to admire the cherry blossoms.

Spring is here. It is time to put the crops in as quickly as possible. The farmer has a new seeder to help him with his spring sowing. The farmer does not have to trudge across his fields broadcasting seeds. His machine drops them in neat rows.

These farmers have come a long way from the backwoods, thanks to technology. A tractor pulls their seeding machine. The tractor replaced plow horses and made farm work easier. The disks on the bottom of the seeder made grooves in the soil. The boxes on top of the machine carry seeds.

Either the scarecrow is very scary and keeps away the birds, or the birds can't find anything to eat in this garden! It is still early in the year. Later in the summer Ms. Scarecrow will have an important job to do. Where do you think her outfit came from?

It is hard for us to imagine the joys of harvest time. The family is proud of their garden crop. They worked so hard in the spring and summer to plant and weed the vegetables. What a reward! The pumpkin crop is especially healthy this fall.

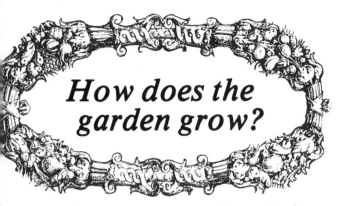

How does the garden grow?

Does your family have a vegetable garden? Do you grow all the vegetables you put on your dinner table? Perhaps you grow only the vegetables you especially like and buy the rest at a store. There were no large grocery stores where the settlers could buy fresh food. If they wanted vegetables they had to grow their own.

The early farmer's garden was much larger than most gardens today. Farmers had to plant, weed, and harvest all the vegetables they needed for the entire year!

Collecting the seeds

Farmers could not go to the local nursery to buy seeds and seedlings the way we do. Settlers brought seeds with them to plant in their garden. Neighbors traded with each other to get new varieties of plants. After the first harvest, families collected seeds from their own vegetables. The seeds were separated and carefully dried. Then they were wrapped in newspaper or cloth and tied with string. The names of the seeds were written on the containers. If the seeds were mixed up, the garden would be unpredictable next

 summer! The seeds had to be stored in a very dry place until the spring. If the seeds were carelessly put in a damp place, they would rot.

The compost heap

Early farmers could not buy chemical fertilizers for their gardens. They made their own fertilizers to be sure that the nutrients used by plants were replaced. A family made a **compost heap.** The word "compost" means a "mixture." The compost was heaped into a wooden bin and kept in the shade of the house. The early farmers did not waste anything! They threw egg shells, pumpkin rinds, potato peels, and the rest of their table scraps into the compost heap. All **organic** leftovers and garbage were put into the bin. Do you know what happened next? All of these scraps slowly decomposed

into a rich fertilizer. In the spring, the farmer mixed some manure with this compost and spread the fertilizer over the garden soil. The garden plants loved this organic food!

Settlers loved vegetables. The farm kitchen was no place for picky eaters. The farm family planted onions, parsnips, lettuce, peas, beans, asparagus, cabbage, beets, carrots, cucumbers, and lots and lots of potatoes. Potatoes were a **staple** food.

For many years settlers thought tomatoes were poisonous. They grew them in their gardens as a decoration, but did not eat them. Later they realized that tomatoes were not only safe, but tasty. The early farmers planted extra pumpkin and squash patches where they grew feed for their cattle and pigs.

Spices and seasonings

Early farmers could not buy spices and seasonings. They grew their own herbs and spices in their gardens. Do you recognize any of the following herbs: rue, thyme, sage, rosemary, savory, fennel, caraway, wormwood, lovage, or pennyroyal? These are some of the flavorful herbs the settlers added to their soups and stews. In the fall, when the herbs were ripe, the farmers picked and dried them. They hung them in little bunches from the pantry ceiling where they were handy to the cook.

The settlers protected their food. Every country garden was surrounded by a sturdy fence to keep out the chickens, pigs, cattle, and rabbits which loved to nibble on the little green shoots. Children enjoyed making a scarecrow to fool the wild pests who could fly over the fence. The fence was lined with hollyhocks, gooseberry, raspberry, and currant bushes.

Private patches for the children

Children helped to tend the garden. Often each child had a private vegetable patch. Children planted the vegetables that they loved best in these little plots. Learning to grow vegetables was an important skill. Do you think you would like your own vegetable patch? Imagine watching vegetables grow from tiny seeds into full-grown plants. What vegetables would you plant in your garden?

There seemed to be as many recipes for apples as there were apples! Settlers made apple pies, cakes, cookies, stuffing, dumplings, crisps, and strudels. Apples could be baked, boiled, and just bitten into. Apple cider refreshed tired and thirsty workers. At the bottom of this picture they are making cider by pressing the apples.

The family enjoys a day in the orchard. Ray, Steve, and Susan are picking apples. Charles and Harold are sorting them. The bruised apples are sent along to Philip, who presses them into the barrel to make cider. Jimmy is admiring the shine!

The beautiful orchard

Farmers were very proud of their orchards. After many years of hard work and patience the sight of the beautiful trees full of fruit was a wonderful reward. The tastes of the apples, cherries, peaches, pears, plums, and quinces were even better!

The young fruit trees had to be tended carefully. They were pruned or trimmed so that the branches grew evenly and the tree was wide rather than tall. The fruit from the trees that grew wild in the new country was small and bitter. If settlers did not bring **saplings** with them, they improved the wild fruit by experimenting in their orchards. This experimenting was called **grafting**. Grafting means taking a branch or **cion** from one fruit tree and attaching it to the limb of a different tree. Some farmers were so skillful that they could graft plum branches onto a peach tree!

Grafting was a delicate operation. It was most often performed in the early spring when the sap ran strongly through the fruit trees. Usually between February and April the weather was mild enough for grafting.

Grafting to improve the fruit

The farmers chose the healthiest branches for cions. Usually the best branches were shoots from the past year's growth. The cions were cut smoothly and carefully. Next, the farmer prepared the tree that would grow the cion. The farmer cut a wedge in the tree to match the shape of the cion. When the cion was fitted into the limb, the pieces fit, as in a puzzle. The farmer coated the new graft with clay or wax. The clay was made of horse dung. Clay was cheaper to use but wax made a better seal for the graft. The wax was made of beef fat and beeswax. The farmer spread this seal on the bark and then wrapped a piece of cloth around the new graft. The two kinds of fruit grew a third variety. A successful farmer could discover a delicious new kind of apple.

The cion

The cion in the tree limb

The bandaged graft

35

Bee-utiful honey!

Settler children loved honey. They searched for their own honey supply. Honeycombs fresh from the hive were a tempting catch!

Baiting the bee

When the flower season was nearly over and the bees had collected their supply of honey for the winter, eager children began the hunt. They placed a small amount of honey in a box to use as bait for a bee. They took their boxes into a field or wood and sat down to wait. Sometimes they burned some honeycomb near the box because the bee would be attracted to the smell. When a bee finally buzzed by, it took honey from the box. It flew off to the hive with its food.

The children ran after the bee but the little insect soon flew out of sight. The children were not discouraged. They knew that bees fly in a straight line. When they were following the "beeline," they knew they were on the right track.

The queen bee

When the children lost sight of the bee, they put down the box of honey, burned more honeycomb, and attracted another bee. They followed this bee until once again they lost sight of it. They patiently tried again.

Finally they discovered the beehive. They tried to remember exactly where the hive was so that they could return later in the year. Sometimes they marked the bark of the tree with an "X." This helped them to find their supply. If other children found the marked tree, they knew the supply was already taken.

Uncovering the hive

On a cold day in the fall the children returned for the honey. They came in the fall because they knew the hive would be overflowing with the honey the bees had stored for the winter. They picked a cold day because bees become lazy and less likely to sting when they are chilly.

If the hive was too high to reach with a stick, the adventurous children cut off the branch where it was built. Sometimes they chopped down the whole tree! They broke the hive. The sticky, sweet honeycomb was revealed. Very carefully, the children put all of the comb into a pail. Sometimes they found a large hive and could fill the whole bucket with honeycomb.

The worker

No doubt many children had bad experiences with bee hunts. These sweet-toothed settler children must have felt that the golden honey was worth the risk of being stung!

Do you think you would like to hunt for beehives in order to get the honey for your morning breakfast? Some settler children were probably quite content simply to pick berries for their mother and enjoy the sweet fruit jam that she made.

Home, sweet home

When a hive became too crowded for comfort, the bees divided in two groups. Half of the bees stayed in their own home, and the homeless half flew off. They swarmed until they found a place to live.

Uncle Louis has taken the roof off one of his beehives. You can see where the bees have built their comb. Each hive is numbered so Uncle Louis can keep track of his bees. The bees have their own addresses! They also have clover blossoming on their doorsteps.

The bees swarm!

Sometimes bees swarmed even when they were not seeking a new hive. Some settlers were afraid of them. Some children rushed to grab pots and pans while others ran to get a mirror. They clattered the pots and pans and used the mirror to reflect sunlight into the swarm. The noise and light were supposed to make the bees think that there was a thunderstorm with lightning. The settlers expected the bees to rush home to their hives to get out of the rain. This trick did not always save the settlers from stings!

The apiary

Farmers sometimes kept their own bees in an **apiary**. The first hand-made hives were often built of straw. Later, farmers made beehives of wood. The apiary looked like a collection of miniature huts.

Collecting the honey crop

Farmers harvested honey in the fall. They often used smoke to kill most of the bees. The farmers covered their skin with clothes and put nets over their heads just in case some of the bees were still alive. They always left some hives alone so that the bee colony would grow and produce more honey the next year.

Basswood blossoms   White clover

Each kind of flowering plant gave a special flavor to the honey the bee made from the nectar. Honey made from white clover was especially sweet and delicate. The blooms of the basswood tree made delicious honey. The flowers of buckwheat plants gave honey an unmistakable taste. The large heads of sunflowers produced so much nectar that farmers sometimes planted them near their apiary.

These chickens do not look very nourishing, but the tramp is determined to catch his dinner. All he plucked was a handful of feathers. Barnyards were raided by wild animals as well as people.

The old gray mare has been "put out to pasture." Her strong son, Bucky, keeps her company when he's not at work pulling the farm wagon.

The barnyard

The animals that lived on the clearings in the backwoods were skinny, bad-tempered, and tough. They were not given shelter in a barn. The settlers had no time to build a barn until after the family had a cabin. The cows and pigs had to hunt for their own food in the bush. The settlers were busy growing food for themselves. They kept only enough animals for the needs of the family. The early settler farm usually had a yoke of sturdy oxen, two or three cows, some calves, about six sheep, a mean old sow, and a litter of pigs.

When the settler had a barn for the animals and plenty of food to feed them, they grew fat and friendly. The settlers were able to keep more animals. They had time to work on improving their stock. Fancy breeds were imported from other countries.

The barnyard was a busy, noisy, happy place. Children helped in the barn and yard. They fed, watered, and cleaned the animals. There was often excitement because new animals were being born. Children took special care of the calves, foals, lambs, and chicks.

The barnyard is bustling. Michael is feeding the poultry. Daniel is mucking out the horse stall. Wilbur is pumping water. Rachel and Father don't know which job to do first!

Rise and shine, Henrietta!

Henrietta was a young settler girl who lived on a farm. She had many chores to do every morning. Before she even had her own breakfast, Henrietta had to feed all the animals in the barnyard. This is a typical morning in the life of Henrietta.

A sunbeam teased Henrietta awake just as the rooster tuned up. It was a beautiful day. The scent of apple blossoms blew through the window. Petals drifted in on the breeze. From the kitchen came the soft thump, thump of bread dough against the board. Mother was already busy!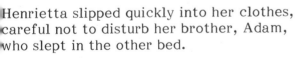

Henrietta slipped quickly into her clothes, careful not to disturb her brother, Adam, who slept in the other bed.

"Good morning, Mother," she whispered when she entered the kitchen. "I am going to let Adam stay in bed awhile. He is tired out with the excitement of having a pet of his own. I can do his chores. Father can wake him when he needs him." She tiptoed to the fireplace and peeked at the baby pig asleep on the hearth. The pig was Adam's new pet. It was sick and needed to be nursed.

Split the kindling and fetch the water

"Very well, Henrietta," her mother smiled. "But we must not spoil him. I will get him up for breakfast. Could you split some more kindling for me, child, and fetch the bucket? I used the last of the water for washing, and the kitchen fire is almost out."

Henrietta was glad to be out in the fresh morning air. She rinsed her face and hands at the well. She skipped back with the bucket of water for Mother, then headed for the barn.

Across the field, she could see Father and the team, Fan and Queen, plowing the land. The sun gleamed on the sweating sides of the horses as their great feet paced the long rows.

Jasper, the dog, caught sight of her, and yapped foolishly. Jasper still acted like a pup. He sometimes forgot that he was a trained sheep dog! Father looked up and waved. Henrietta waved back before ducking into the shady barn.

39

Sunny the sow hardly knows where to put her feet. Whenever she tries to move, there is a piglet underfoot. There are six piglets in the picture, and they are only half of Sunny's litter. Little pigs are playful, but they squirm when you try to hold them.

Clean the stalls and milk the cow

Flossy and Bess mooed with pleasure to see Henrietta. Bess was going to have her first calf any day now. She stepped about nervously as Henrietta hurried around, cleaning the stalls and forking down hay.

"Never mind, Bess. I have a treat for you," soothed Henrietta. She gave Bess a taste of maple sugar and went to milk Flossy. Impatient old Flossy always felt better after she was milked. When Henrietta finished the milking, she split kindling until the ax was dull. Father would sharpen it when he came in for breakfast.

Collect the eggs and put out the sheep

By this time, the feeding of the smaller animals was long overdue. Henrietta threw open the door to the chicken coop. The startled hens cackled and fluttered out into the yard. Henrietta scattered corn in a wide arc. Then she went into the coop to search the twelve nests for eggs. Cluck and Speckle were the best egg layers. Today there were six white eggs. The white eggs would be traded for supplies at the village store. People thought white eggs were better than brown eggs.

Next, Henrietta whistled for Jasper. The dog came running. Henrietta opened the gate to the sheep pen and coaxed the reluctant animals into the yard. From there, Jasper took over, driving the sheep to the meadow to graze.

"Nearly through," panted Henrietta as she arrived back at the house and gave her mother the precious eggs. Then she gathered the feed for Sunny and ran to the pigpen. She stood on the bottom rail of the pen and peered through the bars.

Slop the hog and feed the poultry

"How are you today, new mother?" she sang, and then laughed out loud. Sunny the sow lay on her side. She seemed to be pinned in place by twelve tiny pigs. She raised her head, gave a hungry sigh, and settled back again. Henrietta dumped the slop of porridge, bread, and sour milk into Sunny's trough.

"Never mind your manners, Sunny. I can see that you are tied down."

Henrietta hurries to the house with kindling for the stove. She works hard at her morning chores. She is trying to remember all of the little jobs that must be done.

Curly is a **ram.** He is the only male sheep on the farm. He is the father of all the lambs which are born every spring. He is on the lookout for wolves who want to eat his flock.

Beefy is a bull. He works at being a good father to beef calves. He plays at scaring the daring children who take short cuts through his pasture.

The cattle are wading into the river for a drink. They are allowed to roam the pasture to find the best spots for grazing. In the winter the farmer feeds them hay made from grass and clover that he has cut and dried.

Thank you, pretty cow

Thank you, pretty cow, that made
Pleasant milk to soak my bread,
Every day and every night,
Warm, and fresh, and sweet, and white.

Do not chew the hemlock rank,
Growing on the weedy bank,
But the yellow cowslips eat,
They will make it very sweet!

Where the purple violet grows,
Where the bubbling water flows,
Where the grass is fresh and fine,
Pretty cow, go there and dine.

The children help in the field whenever there is planting or picking to be done. They were going to finish plowing, but had to mend a piece of harness first.

Just outside the barn the turkeys, ducks, and geese waited for the crumbs and crushed Indian corn Henrietta had hidden in her pail. She left the chore of feeding this bunch until last. She wished these birds were as resourceful as the guinea hens at finding their own food. Then she would never have to go near those nasty geese! More than once these vicious fowl have pushed her down on the ground. She grabbed a stick from her pile of kindling and braced herself for an attack. The geese hardly noticed her today! They were much more interested in the contents of her pail. Twaddle, her favorite duck, followed her around and nipped at her ankles. It was his way of saying, "Thank you for a delicious breakfast."

Breakfast at last!

Mother was striking the bake kettle with a wooden spoon. This was the signal to come and eat. Adam was helping Mother by carefully turning the flapjacks. Father said a short prayer and everyone sat down. There were bowls of porridge, plenty of fresh eggs, milk, bread, and flapjacks with maple syrup.

A surprise

After breakfast, Adam fed his pet pig while Mother and Henrietta did the dishes. Father sharpened the ax. Then the whole family gathered in the field to do the planting. By the time they returned, the shadows were getting long. Father went to the barn to unhitch the team. A moment later he came running back as fast as his barn boots could carry him.

"Jane," he called. "Come and see. Bess has had a fine bull calf. We can trade him." Father turned to Henrietta and Adam. "And how would you two little helpers like a pony?" he said.

43

Linda thinks that lambs make the best farm pets. Her father does not sell the sheep for meat. When Linda's pet lamb grows up, its coat will be used to make woolen clothes for the family. Linda loves to take care of the lambs which are born every spring. The lamb seems to be smiling along with Linda!

Shearing sheep

Settlers kept sheep because their wool could be made into so many things. The settlers could knit or weave blankets, shirts, dresses, hats, socks, and sweaters from wool. Without woolen clothing, they might have frozen during the long, cold winters.

Farmers **sheared** the wool from their sheep in the spring. As soon as it was warm enough, all the sheep were herded into a nearby stream to have a bath. After being outside in the mud, the sheep were filthy! It took a day or two for the sheep to dry off after they were washed in the stream because wool soaks up water.

A close shave!

Shearing never hurt the sheep, but they still did not enjoy it much. Imagine someone holding you down and clipping all your hair off with giant shears! When the sheep's wool was full of bugs or ticks, a solution made from tobacco leaves was applied to kill them. This solution also helped to heal any cuts caused by the farmer's hand slipping. Can you picture how different the sheep would look after all their fluffy wool had been sheared off?

After all the sheep were sheared the wool was sorted carefully. Lumps of dirt and burrs sticking in the wool were removed. The wool was then spread out on a clean floor. Melted lard was sprinkled over it. Why do you think the wool was greased? If you feel the wool on a sheep you will notice that it is wiry. Greasing the wool makes it soft and flexible. After the wool was greased, farmers used a special rod to whip the wool into shape.

Finally the wool was ready. Some settlers used bleach to make it snowy white before they **carded** it. Carding combed the hairs so that they could be formed into a thread and spun. Soon there were many skeins of beautiful wool.

Minnie puts up a fight

Farmers often had a big problem because wolves killed their sheep. A mean, hungry pack of wolves could kill more than ten sheep in one night. Here is the story of one girl determined to protect her pet lamb:

"My sister had a pet lamb. Minnie and her lamb were the best of friends. One afternoon Minnie was going down to the spring for a pail of water. She saw a large dog (or thought she did) worrying her pet lamb. Minnie, being naturally courageous, picked up a large stick and struck the beast two or three times with all her strength. The beast was forced to drop Minnie's favorite lamb. This, however, he did very reluctantly. He turned his head at the same time as he let go of the lamb, and showed his teeth with a most devilish snarl.

That "dog" is a wolf!

"When the beast looked at Minnie, she stopped short. She could tell by his pricked ears, high cheekbones, long bushy tail, and bony body, that her enemy was not a dog. He was a wolf! But there was nothing that would stop Minnie. She bravely attacked the wolf again. She followed him down by the creek, thrashing him and calling for help with all her might. Finally I heard her cries. At once I grabbed my gun and rushed toward her. When the wolf saw the reinforcement, he scampered off with all his speed."

Mittens hated being sheared, but she suddenly feels nice and cool. Look at that coat!

Button takes longer than usual giving herself a bath on Blaze's back. The cat loves to tease the dog when she's out of reach! Blaze is a saddle horse, not a workhorse. He is small compared to the gigantic workhorses on the farm. Owning a horse especially for riding was a luxury.

*King and Mr. Draper are competing in a plowing match against other draft horses and their owners. They will win the contest if they plow **furrows** the straightest and fastest.*

The giants of the farm

The kings and queens of the settler farm were the workhorses. These gigantic beasts were beautiful. They had powerful shoulders and huge heads with Roman noses. They had fans of hair around their hooves called "horse-feathers." Sitting on plow horses felt like sitting on top of the world. Their backs were so broad it seemed as if you could make your bed up there! Cats especially loved to perch on the plow horses where they could calmly clean themselves without any interruptions.

The workhorses might look dangerous, but they were usually as gentle as kittens. They did not mind at all when the children took them for a ride even though it was the horses' time off. Children simply had to be careful they did not fall under the big feet.

Even the names of the kinds of plow horses sound powerful. Settlers owned breeds called Percherons, Belgians, and Clydesdales. You have probably seen these giants pulling wagons. They are called draft horses. "Draft" is an adjective used to describe things that can pull heavy loads.

The farmer had a special relationship with the workhorses. During the seasons of planting and harvest, the farmer worked with the horses all day long. The farmer and the horses understood special signals. When the farmer said "Gee," the horses turned quickly to the right. "Haw" made the horses swerve to the left. You can guess what "Whoa" and "Giddup" meant.

Duchess is still far too small to pull the plow. Louise thinks she is just the right size.

Betty's chicks have just hatched. They are still awkward and confused. The chick on the right seems to think he's still an egg!

Squawk! These puppies have just been born. How are they to know the difference between mother's milk and chicken feathers?

Barnyard birds

Chickens, geese, guinea hens, turkeys, and the occasional peacock made their home in the barnyard. These birds are called **poultry.** Farmers used their eggs and flesh for food.

These birds could be a nuisance. They were trespassers! They helped themselves to the grain that was stored in the barn. When hens were not kept in a coop, they laid their eggs all over the barn. It was quite a chore to search for eggs in the morning.

The geese loved to sneak into the garden to steal fresh, young vegetables. Farmers sometimes put large collars around the necks of the geese so they could not poke their heads through the garden fence.

Chickens, sometimes called **fowl,** were very important to the settlers' survival. Farmers usually built chicken coops where their hens could roost and lay their eggs. The coop kept wild animals from stealing the eggs and kept the chickens from stealing the food from the family.

Fowl food

Fowl would eat almost anything. They usually picked at seeds scattered in the barnyard. Chickens added spice to their diet by eating worms, maggots, and grasshoppers. What foul food! Feeding the hens boiled potatoes made them healthy and plump. In the winter farmers fed their chickens crushed bones. Calcium was good for the hens.

You have probably heard the phrase "running around like a chicken with its head cut off." When it was time to kill a bird for food, its head was chopped off. For a short time, the chicken's nervous system continued to direct the movement of the chicken. What a sight it was to see the chicken's body flapping about without its head!

Farmers created strange kinds of chickens through breeding. Some have mops of feathers on their heads. Others have overgrown combs. Can you find the turkeys, ducks, rabbits, and pigeons in the picture? The bird in the bottom right corner is a guinea hen.

Workers check eggs for red spots before they send them to city markets. A red spot means that the egg has been fertilized and cannot be sent to market. A chick could have grown in a fertilized egg if the egg had not been taken from the warmth of the nest.

Geese could give you goose bumps. You might find your goose cooked if you were going to visit friends and met a gaggle of geese at the gate. Geese made a terrible racket honking and hissing, and their bites were as bad as their barks!

Can Tracy save Porky? She was on her way to feed her pet pig and found him surrounded. The geese think they own the bridge over their creek. Porky sure is paying the toll for crossing the bridge!

The geese guard the yard

A flock of geese greeting visitors at the gate could be frightening. Geese often behaved like guard dogs. When strangers approached, geese made a terrible noise, honking and hissing as they waddled as fast as their flat feet could carry them. Strangers had to steer clear of their big bills. Geese could give them nasty bites!

When plucking day came these brave birds turned into a sorry sight. They knew it was "that time of the year" again when the farmer put them in the pens overnight. The farmer wanted their feathers to be dry.

The feathers fly

One by one the geese were caught. Their heads were covered in an old sock so they could not bite. Plucking did not hurt them very much, but it hurt their pride. The big feathers were used for pillows and mattresses. The tiny "pin" feathers were saved to stuff pillows for babies. Nothing could be more downy than a goose-feather pillow.

By the time plucking was finished, the yard looked as if a snowstorm had swept through. Bits of down floated in the air like snowflakes. The geese huddled in the corner of the yard, nursing what was left of their ruffled feathers.

Helen is dry but the geese made her cry!

51

The family milk cow has won first prize at the fair. Missy is just glad to be home where there is peace and quiet after spending the day at the noisy, dusty fairgrounds. She especially likes being fed from Margy's hand.

*These three **heifers** are resting in the pasture. Heifers are young cows that have not yet given birth to calves.*

How now, brown cow

The milk cow deserved to be pampered. She gave the settler family all the fresh milk they could drink. Without the dependable old cow there was no thick cream, no sweet butter, no tangy buttermilk, and no delicious cheese. Each family had a favorite name for their milk cow, whether she was called Buttercup or Bessy, Missy or Flossy.

The milk cow demanded attention, and the job of looking after her was one of the most important chores on the farm. She had to be milked every morning and every night. She needed fresh green grass or fine tender hay. Molasses was a special treat, and gave the milk a sweet flavor. If the milk cow had a lunch of onions, her milk would taste like onion soup!

The following story, **Amy learns the ropes**, describes a city girl's experiences with a milk cow.

Amy and her family are welcomed to Uncle Donald's farm. Amy is going to stay all summer. Amy is not even sure that she likes the chicks! Wait until she meets Bossy, the milk cow.

Amy learns the ropes

Amy was looking forward to visiting her Uncle Donald's farm. It was a long journey to get here, but she would be staying for the whole summer. She was eager to see the pigs and horses, to collect eggs from the henhouse, and, most of all, to learn how to milk a cow. Her cousins, Raymond and Patsy, were almost Amy's own age, and they promised to teach their "city cousin" all about life on a farm.

Amy's Uncle Donald was the first to demonstrate to her how a cow was milked. He told Amy that milking was a skill which took practice to perfect. The sturdy little three-legged stool was positioned just right. Uncle Donald rested his head against Bossy's belly, wiggling his fingers to warm them up. The milk pail was placed under the cow's **udder**. Uncle Donald spoke softly to Bossy, then sang her a song so that she would relax and not kick. Amy was fascinated. The large animal was so contented when Uncle Donald milked her.

Amy soon felt at home on the farm. Now she welcomes the chicks into the world. She found them hatching in an old cupboard.

53

Raymond can milk Bossy easily. Uncle Donald thinks that milking Bossy in the barnyard is funny. Raymond would be surprised if Bossy suddenly decided to take a walk.

Amy jumped away from the cow in surprise. She had just been slapped by Bossy's tail! The milk spills. If at first you don't succeed, try, try again!

The thirsty cats come running

As soon as the barn cats saw that the milking was about to begin, they came running from all directions, mewing and crying. The farmer held two teats, one in each hand, and squeezed and pulled firmly and regularly. "It's almost like a soda fountain!" thought Amy.

The milk sprayed out in a strong stream, ringing against the pail. Uncle Donald paused now and again to aim the milk at the cats, who did not mind being covered with milk. They would immediately lick themselves clean.

Amy could hardly wait to learn how to milk Bossy! Bright and early the next day, Raymond and Patsy woke Amy to give her the first lesson. Raymond perched on the stool near Bossy's belly, took her teats, and began to milk.

"Now that I've started the milking," said Raymond, "you finish up!"

Don't cry over spilt milk!

How large and imposing old Bossy seemed to Amy when she sat beneath her, but Amy had carefully watched her uncle and cousin. She believed she would have no problems! What a shock poor Amy got when, just as she grabbed Bossy to begin, the cow's thick tail whipped into her face! Amy jumped up in surprise, spilling the milk already in the pail! Bossy was obviously comfortable with Uncle Donald, the farmer, but was very nervous with strangers. When Amy tried again to get some milk, she avoided Bossy's tail, but could not coax a trickle of milk from the teat.

"Don't worry Amy," said cousin Patsy. "You can try again tomorrow. Bossy has to get to know people before she lets them take her milk." Patsy finished the milking.

"You'll just have to earn her trust," Raymond said. "Don't worry, though. Bossy is always rough with strangers. Sometimes she even kicks over the bucket of milk herself. Of course, our cats love that trick, but then there is no milk for breakfast."

How could Amy earn the trust of a cow? She could not share her secrets or play games with an animal friend as she would with her city friends.

Aunt Beatrice enjoys doing the milking. Milking Bossy gives Aunt Beatrice a chance to get away from it all. She loves this time of day. The sun is rising, the grass sparkles with dew, the cock is crowing, and all the animals are eager to greet her.

Amy tries the sugar-cube trick

The next morning, Amy brought sugar cubes to Bossy. "Maybe the way to a cow's heart is through her stomach," she laughed. Bossy ate the cubes quickly, but Amy still could not coax any milk from her. How could Uncle Donald, Raymond, and Patsy make it look so easy?

That evening, Amy left the barn empty-handed again. She had even brushed down Bossy in the afternoon. That cow was just plain stubborn.

That night, a fierce thunderstorm hit the countryside. Everyone remained inside the big farmhouse. Uncle Donald read by candle-light. Amy and Patsy worked on some shirts that needed mending. Lightning flashed across the sky. The hound dog shook with fright. Raymond petted him, trying to soothe his jumpy nerves.

"That's it!" cried Amy, as she ran to her bunk. She left a surprised group and went out to the barn carrying a blanket and a lantern.

Bossy becomes a friend

Inside the barn, Bossy was pacing back and forth. She was used to sleeping outside in the pasture. Bossy did not like being kept in the barn overnight. Not only that, she was frightened by the sound of the thunder. Amy petted and talked to Bossy to relax her. Amy sat down on the edge of the manger to wait for the storm to pass. Bossy began to look contented. Soon the cow lay down. She looked ready to fall asleep. When the storm let up, Amy crept back to the farmhouse.

The next day, Amy attempted once again to milk Bossy. Bossy "mooed" at Amy and suddenly Amy knew she had the right touch. The two became fast friends. Patsy and Raymond were proud of their cousin.

"Who says a 'city slicker' can't milk a cow?" boasted Amy.

Buster the dog figures this pig has no right to hog his doghouse. The pig was feeling quite comfortable in his new home until Buster dragged him out by his ear. Some of the other pigs are peeking over the fence of their pen. They are enjoying the fight between Buster and the hog.

Pig tales

The pigs raised by the early settlers were so skinny that they were called "razorbacks." They ran so fast that they were called "wind-splitters." They were so ugly with their big heads and long bodies that they were called "alligators." They ran wild in the bush. When the pigs were too fast to catch, the farmer often hunted them with a gun. Farmers joked that pigs were so skinny they had to tie a knot in their tails to stop them from slipping through fences. If a farmer wanted to fatten them before the slaughter, he fed them Indian corn and peas. Children were often terrified of the beasts. Pigs were as nimble as goats and would eat anything from table scraps to snakes. They especially liked buttermilk, potato skins, acorns, and the eggs of birds whose nests were on the ground.

The early farmers often let their pigs run wild in the bush. The pigs were hard to catch. Rob has tamed a few of them by sharing his lunch.

The sow snores while her babies have supper. The piglets pile up and dig in! The pigs on the lower level are too hungry to tell the others to get off their backs.

"Supper's coming. You look over the fence and I'll look through it." These pigs can't keep their eyes off their food. Lynne has a pail of table scraps for them.

The old goat

Agatha has twins. Topsy figures that he is king of the castle. Turvy is too hungry even to notice.
Goats are mischievous creatures. They like to butt people from behind. Some farmers kept goats
because they enjoyed goat's milk and cheese.

The farmer's best friend

"Come on, Casey. It's time to get the sheep!" Casey lifts his ears. "Sheep" is a word he knows. Off he runs to help Ben corral the pesky creatures.

Casey, the farm dog, is a mutt. Most farmers will tell you that mutts make the best farm dogs. Casey is a valuable guard dog and a hard worker. Yesterday, little Betsy wandered away into the forest while the older children picked berries. Casey's keen nose tracked her scent until she was found, safe and sound.

The farm feline

Everyone was grateful. Casey was allowed to sleep beside Ben's bed for the night. Usually he sleeps in the woodhouse during the summer. In the winter, Casey sleeps behind the warm kitchen stove. Sometimes the cat challenges him for this warm bed behind the stove. Max is the only house cat on the farm. The rest of the cats have to live in the barn and catch rats and mice for their meals. Max is a fat cat. Once in a while he waltzes down to the barn at milking time to share a bowl of warm milk with the other cats.

Today, it is business as usual. Casey chases rabbits out of the garden and catches stray pigs that have escaped from the pen. He jogs along beside Ben when he goes to round up the cattle. Casey runs after the big animals, nipping at their heels and herding them toward the barn. He barks to warn Mother that a stranger is coming. This time, it is not a tramp or a thief. The stranger is a hungry traveler.

Turn that churn!

One of Casey's hardest jobs is churning the butter. Many farmers churn their butter by hand, but Mr. Smythe has rigged up a treadmill attached to the churn. When Casey walks on the treadmill, he turns the churn. Fastened to the treadmill, Casey marches on and on until his tongue hangs out because of the heat. At last the butter is ready and Casey can rest.

Mother gives him a big slice of bread and fresh butter. How good it tastes! Now it is time for Casey's nap.

People taking short cuts through a farmer's field could damage crops. Rip will make sure that no one tramples on his master's barley.

The barn cat has found his way into the house. Kit wishes the cat could stay. Father explains that Felix has a job to do catching rats.

59

The family's only horse has died from a disease called "hippozymosis." Even the veterinarian could not help. He said the disease was spreading across the country. In some cases it made humans sick.

Who will make the first move? A fox has surprised some wild rabbits. The rabbits were helping themselves to the farmer's crop. The fox is going to help himself to the rabbits. Wild animals caused problems for farmers.

Dreams and disappointments

The story of many early farmers is a story about hard work, courage, and success. Men, women, and children labored all day long just to grow enough to feed themselves. Their hard work was rewarded. Crops ripened in the sun. Animals were born in the clean, warm barn. The farm life was joyful.

The story of many early farmers is also a story about heartbreak and failure. Farming was never a holiday. Sometimes farming was a disaster. Often farmers could not afford to replace animals that became sick and died. When a family's only workhorse died, the family lost most of the crops that were planted. There was no way to bring in all of the harvest before it rotted in the fields. In one day, bad weather or crop diseases could wipe out the family's food supply. What the family could save from disease and bad weather was often destroyed by wild animals.

Some farmers were forced to give up their dreams of independence and a wonderful family life. They moved to the cities to find jobs. For some, the dream of owning a farm turned into a nightmare.

This farmer has double trouble. A wicked storm is blowing up and the pigs are eating his pumpkins.

Fire sweeps toward the farmer's land. He must plow around his field to save his grain from flames.

Hallelujah for the harvest!

Gail lends Father a hand, and her help is appreciated even if her helping hands are small. Father is cutting oats with the horses and reaper. Gail is trying to tie the bundles of grain into sheaves.

Grandpa holds his **scythe** upside-down to sharpen it. Scythes were used to cut grain and hay before machines were invented to do the job. Grandpa has been cutting grass for hay. It is full of daisies.

The entire family has helped to stack the bundles or **sheaves** of wheat into upright piles called **stooks.** The baby, Pam, sits on top of a stook. The grain is piled in the field to dry in the sun.

Millie wears a big hat to protect her from the sun while she works in the field. She sits on the **mower** behind the horsepower. This field will make rich hay when the clover is cut and dried.

Reaping, flailing, winnowing, and grinding

Harry rocks the **cradle** to cut oats. The cradle replaced the **scythe**. The scythe has a blade with a long handle. The cradle has wooden bars added to the handle of the blade. The bars catch and cradle the grain when it is cut. When a load of stalks collects on the cradle, the farmer can drop the grain into neat, straight piles.

Luke is using a **flail**. The flail beats the heads of wheat from their stalks. Farmers used flails for centuries until threshing machines were invented. Luke swings the flail by its long wooden pole. A shorter, thicker piece of wood is attached to the pole with metal rings and leather straps. The shorter pole swings in all directions.

Sam is **winnowing** wheat. After the grain has been flailed, the heads of wheat are put into this big tray. When Sam shakes the tray, the **chaff** of the wheat is separated from the grains. The wind blows the chaff away from the grains. Chaff makes you itchy. Harry hopes the chaff will not fly in his face.

Grains of wheat are being poured into a **quern**. The quern grinds the grain. The quern is made of two flat, round stones. One stone sits on top of the other. The bottom stone does not move. The top stone is turned by the wooden handle as the grain is poured through the hole. The grain is ground into coarse flour between the stones.

These boys provide the power for a little threshing machine by turning a wheel. The belt attached to the wheel makes the machine work. The machine spins the heads of grain away from the stalks.

My diary: threshing day

Today was threshing day! We were up early so we would have time to eat enough to keep us going until dinner. Breakfast was wonderful. We had berries and cream with buttermilk biscuits. Mama made the biscuits fresh and hot and buttery. Then came mounds of scrambled eggs and great slices of ham. Father kept telling us to eat, eat, eat! "Can't get the job done on an empty stomach," he said, and shoveled another mound of eggs onto our plates.

I was the waterboy. It's not a fancy job but Father says I'm only eight. Mama says keeping the workers watered is one of the most important jobs on threshing day. I like the way she says that, as if the men were plants! When I took the big jug to the men, they joked with me and patted my head. They slung the jug over one arm and took gigantic gulps. One man practically drank a whole jugful, and there were twelve of them in the field. I wore a path in the grass going back and forth to and from the well.

The threshing contraption

All our neighbors use the same threshing machine. It's a funny contraption. The horses are hitched to a treadmill. They walk all day and go nowhere! The treadmill is attached to the thresher by belts. The belts turn the **cylinder.** The men feed the stalks of grain into the cylinder. Everything gets dumped in a mess at the other end, and more men work pitching the straw in a pile and shoveling the grain into sacks. I guess this is what "threshing" means. Some people say "thrashing." The words are the same. They mean that the grain is thrashed away from the stalk. Father sometimes threatens to give me a "thrashing" when I am bad. He never does, but I guess this word is the same too.

Beating out the grain

Father says until a few years ago they used a flail to thrash grain. It must have been hard work. The old flail is hung up in the barn. It's just a big stick attached to a shorter stick by a piece of leather. You hold the big stick, and the shorter stick swings around and thrashes the stalks until all the heads fall off. "Flail" is a funny word. Mama says it means the same as thrash. Father never says he will flail me, but I suppose he could use this word too.

Horses pull around in a circle to power the threshing machine. The threshing machine shakes the grain from the stalks and deposits the grain in a bin at the front of the machine. Straw blows out the back of the thresher. The men store the grain in sacks made of cloth.

These horses are walking on a treadmill. They keep moving all day but they never get anywhere. The belt around the wheel on the side of the treadmill turns the threshing machine, which is outside the barn. Straw is pitched into the mow.

A tractor has taken over the job of the horses. Power from a steam engine runs the thresher. Grain can be harvested faster because the tractor never needs to take a rest. The horses are still needed to pull the loaded wagons to the barn.

Food for the hungry workers

don't mean to write about food all the time, but dinner was so good I never wanted it to end. At noon Mama rang the dinner bell. The men sure looked happy to hear it. They all came trampling into the kitchen. Mama says every family tries to serve the best meal at threshing time. I'm sure Mama's was the best. Even the men pretended that they thought the table was going to collapse under the load. The main course was wonderful enough, but oh, the pies and cakes for dessert were even better! Mama had five pies of apple, and three kinds of cake. She cut the pies in four. These were huge pieces, and still most of the men had two helpings and then packed in cake too!

After dinner, it was back to work. I was running after water until I thought my legs would break and my arms fall off. The men sweated so much that their shirts were all wet, but with all the water they drank I'm not surprised! It is hot, hard work. The chaff of the grain is as prickly as a thistle and as itchy as poison ivy. The men were awfully tired by sunset. I think maybe it is the easiest job being a waterboy. Even so, I'll sleep like a log tonight.

Everyone in the family helps in the fields on threshing day. Anna forks sheaves of oats onto the wagon. Jeff stacks the sheaves. When the wagon is full, they will drive it to the thresher.

The prairie: wheat fields and ranching

Can you imagine driving all of these horses and donkeys? Can you even count them all? They are pulling the machine that reaps the huge fields of prairie wheat. The driver hopes that none of the donkeys decides to be stubborn.

Prairie farmers with wagons loaded with wheat have a long wait at the grain elevator. The grain is stored in the elevator until it is taken by train to the market. These prairie landmarks are called elevators because the grain is elevated and stored at different levels in the tall buildings.

Ranchers look over their herd of cattle. Grazing land on the prairie was rarely fenced. The cattle roamed far and wide. When the cowboys wanted to capture them, they searched them out and rounded them up.

This wild-eyed steer has been roped and tied. Cowboys were experts at roping cattle with lassos. Their horses were trained to stand still with the ropes tied to the saddles. All ranchers had special brands to mark their cattle. If a steer did not have a brand, any cowboy could claim it.

Slaughtering hogs is not much fun, but it's a job that must be done.

Butchering in the fall

In the fall, the early farmers had to butcher their own livestock for meat. After the pigs and cattle were killed, the **carcasses** were hung on the hooks and **gutted.**

The settlers did not waste any part of the animal. They cut thick steaks from beef. They loved to eat roasted spareribs and backbones. They smoked ham and used the fatty sections of the pig for bacon. The settlers saved both the small and large intestines of pigs to use as casings for sausage. They made sausage from the leanest leftover scraps of meat and from the liver and lungs. All the fat was saved too. Fat made good lard for baking. The meat from the heads and feet of pigs was chopped very fine to make **headcheese.** Settlers also used the kidneys of pork and beef for food.

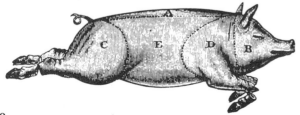

Smoking the meat

The early farmers did not have freezers where they could store their meat. They preserved meat by smoking it in a special building called a **smokehouse.** The smokehouse was built of logs. The cracks in the walls were sealed with clay so the smokehouse was airtight. First, the farmers packed the roasts, ribs, steaks, and other cuts of meat in salt. Salt seasoned and helped to preserve the meat. The meat was hung from the smokehouse rafters.

In the middle of the dirt floor of the building was a small pit. The settlers built a fire in this pit. The smokehouse fire was not like the crackling flames in the farmhouse fireplace. The settlers tried to make the fire smoke by burning chips of hickory wood and apple-tree logs. Hickory and apple smoke had a sweet smell which flavored the meat. After about five days in the smokehouse the meat could be taken down from the rafters. It was ready to eat or to store for the winter.

Cattle on this ranch have been rounded up by cowboys. They are beef cattle. Some of them will be sent to market. On small farms in the early days many farmers did their slaughtering at home. One animal provided the family with enough beef to last the winter.

These cattle are being shipped across the sea from England to farmers who raise beef cattle. They are lowered into the hold below the deck. At the end of their long journey they will be purchased by farmers who want to improve their herds with new breeds.

Facts about farming

Poultry scratched the ground looking for seeds. In the winter, it was so cold that the claws on their feet were frostbitten. Some chickens even lost their toes!

Farmers put metal rings through the noses of their pigs to stop them from rooting underneath fences.

Farmers joked that pigs were so skinny they had to tie knots in their tails to keep them from slipping through fences.

Did you know that early farmers made "coffee" from peas, barley, acorns, and dandelion roots?

A duck would stop laying as soon as it had a nest full of eggs, but if the farmer took each egg after it was laid, a duck would continue to lay more.

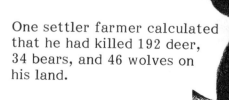

One settler farmer calculated that he had killed 192 deer, 34 bears, and 46 wolves on his land.

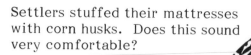

Settlers stuffed their mattresses with corn husks. Does this sound very comfortable?

Settlers made horse collars by braiding corn husks.

Do you know what farm donkeys liked to eat? Thistles! You could call that a "sharp tongue"! Ouch!

Do you know where the word "beeline" came from? When bees finished collecting nectar they headed in a straight line for the hive.

An important source of meat for the early settlers was the black squirrel.

Settlers built little houses over cold water spring The spring kept the house cool. Settlers stored their ice supply in these ice houses.

In the winter, farmers put manure in big piles so that it would not freeze. In the summer they watered the manure pile when it became too dry. They turned the manure with a fork when it smoked from the heat. Manure was precious because it was a good fertilizer.

One farmer noticed that the oats around the family outhouse grew higher than they did in the field! Can you guess why? This fact proved the importance of fertilizer.

Early farmers used a tool that looked like a gigantic, heavy rolling pin pulled by oxen. They rolled this log over their fields to pack down the surface of new meadows, cover broadcasted seeds, and crush clods of earth.

Farmers used their farm wagons to go to church. They simply added boards for seats.

The first farm wagons had wooden **axles** reinforced with a strip of iron. These wheels creaked and soon became stiff. Farmers carried grease for the wagon wheels when they went on long trips. The grease was made with pine pitch. The pitch was mixed with lard in the winter so that it would not be too thick.

Farmers sometimes had apprentices working on their farms. The apprentice worked with the farmer for five or six years. At the end of the apprenticeship, the apprentice was usually given two suits of clothes, a yoke of oxen, a cow and calf, but no money or land.

One settler got lost in the bush with his ox. He did not know what to do. He grabbed the tail of his ox and the ox led him home.

Some settlers believed that if they kept goats with their cows or horses the goats would keep the other animals from getting sick.

The early farmer sometimes made harnesses for his horses from the bark of elm and basswood trees.

A few farmers made their own lime. They heaped limestone on a frame made on large logs. They set fire to the heap at the end of the day. Next morning the stone had been burned into lime. A week later the coals were cool enough to be collected. Lime was used to make whitewash and was used for plastering.

Settler children made "nest eggs" out of clay. They formed them in the same shape as real eggs. Then they painted them with whitewash. These eggs were put into chicken nests. The hens felt them, took the hint, and laid real eggs.

Eggs could be preserved in water mixed with a lump of lime. They could also be kept for a long time when they were packed in salt. When eggs were transported to the cities, they were packed in barrels of oatmeal, not in cardboard cartons.

Mother hands Father a basket of her best apples. She picked and polished each one carefully. She hopes to win a prize for them at the fair. The family has been busy all morning sorting the best of the farm produce for the competitions.

The country fair

Fairs gave farmers a chance to show off their crops and livestock. The best farm products and animals were awarded prizes. Many communities held fairs in the spring and in the fall. Fairs could last from one day to six days. The fairs were important because farmers could meet to talk about improving their crops and animals.

Early on the morning of the fair day, farmers packed their best crops into the wagons. The healthiest animals were lovingly washed and brushed until they were shining clean. Some people took farm animals and produce to sell at the fair. The family kitchen was filled with the smell of pies and cakes.

Mother packed up her most beautiful embroidery and needlepoint. Everyone climbed into the loaded farm wagon, and it creaked off down the road to the bustling fair grounds.

A tour of the fairgrounds

Mr. Thompson is one of the judges at a fair. He has been a judge for the past twenty years. He has a keen eye for detail. You can't fool him! All the farmers respect his decisions and know that he will make his choices honestly and carefully. The judges are touring the exhibits. This year Mr. Thompson is taking his youngest son, Robert, with him on his rounds. The judge wants to teach Robert what to look for in a winner.

Horses of all shapes and sizes crowd one corner of the fairgrounds. The biggest horses in the picture are workhorses. They will be competing in a plowing match in the afternoon. Many of the saddle horses will be running in the race.

Judging the horses

Robert and the judge head over to the animal stalls first. They are going to choose the finest stallion in the county. This is a difficult decision because all fifteen stallions are beauties! The judge shows Robert how to assess each stallion's **conformation.** The legs must be strong and well-formed. Robert and the judge feel each stallion's shiny coat. The texture must be as soft as silk. They check to see if the stallion's eyes are bright and alert. They pry into his mouth to examine his teeth.

After checking each horse, the judge and Robert put their heads together. They both agree that the best horse is a tall, black stallion. The other judges agree too! Robert does the honors by placing a "First Prize" ribbon on Thundercloud. Thundercloud nuzzles Robert as if he is saying "thank you."

Peter is going to enter his young bull in the fair competition. Baron needs a good grooming before he will be ready for the show.

Those filthy pigs!

Robert and the judge must hurry on to the other animal exhibits. Chickens, pigs, cattle, and sheep must all be judged differently. The lambs are Robert's favorites. The pigs do not seem to realize that they should be on their best behavior. They cannot resist a roll in the mud before showtime.

Robert finds that judging grain is interesting. Wheat, oats, barley, and rye are very different from one another. Everyone recognizes corn, but the other grains also have particular sizes, colors, shapes, tastes, and smells.

The test of taste

Robert thinks that testing food is the best task. Robert knows naturally the tastes of the best butter, cheese, and maple sugar. He can tell a good apple from a bad apple! Both Mr. Thompson and Robert find it hard to decide which cake is best. Another sample may help! Robert feels it is a toss-up between Mrs. Smythe's Black Bottom Chocolate Cherry Cake and Mrs. Bell's Deep and Delicious Strawberry Cheesecake. Robert and his father try both cakes just one more time. It's a tie! Both cakes get first prize.

There are many other categories. The judges give ribbons for the best sewing, embroidery, and handmade quilts. In the afternoon they will give a prize to the farmer who plows faster and straighter than anyone else.

The center of this picture shows a busy fairground. Fairs became big and exciting events. People came from the cities and the country to attend them. This large community has a handsome gate leading into the fair. There are permanent sheds to shelter the animals. This fair

SPANISH MERINOS.

SOUTH DOWNS.

...RDS THE ENTRANCE

...RT-HORNED BULL

SHORT HORNED COWS.

lasts six days. Each year the farmers put up huge tents to make room for all of the exhibits. During the fair, the farmers proudly display their accomplishments. You can see some of the breeds of sheep, cattle, and goats that the farmers have entered into the competitions. Some fairs also had writing competitions. The farmer who wrote the best advice about improving animals or crops won a prize.

A growing concern

Do you live on a farm? Many people today have not experienced life on the farm. Most people today live in towns and cities. They shop at big grocery stores where their food is stacked in bright, neat packages. City people may keep a few pets, but most of the animals they see live in a zoo. Many of us do not even think about the life of the people who raise crops and animals for us to eat.

In the early days of this country, almost everyone grew up on a farm. Families planted their own food. Often they sold animals and crops at the local market. In the "good old days," farms were small and crops were harvested with simple tools.

Progress on the farm

There has been a great deal of progress made on the farm since the days of the settlers. Farmers have become so efficient that fewer and fewer of them are needed to feed those of us who live in towns and cities. They have improved methods of crop rotation, fertilization, and irrigation. They have better breeds of plants and animals. They know how to prevent diseases.

Children who grow up on a farm today often move to the city. The farm does not need many "hands" because machines are able to do more work faster. The children who do stay to work the farm often attend agricultural schools to learn farming skills. Farming is a complex business today. Even when you grow up on a farm there are many skills you need to learn before you can manage your land and livestock properly.

The modern methods

Some farmers feel that their way of life is disappearing. Many small farms can no longer support a family. Owners of small farms find it hard to compete against the larger farms. Many family farms have been sold. Suburbs and cities are built where farmers once lived and worked. Today, ranchers patrol huge herds of beef cattle from helicopters. Cowboys on horseback once rounded up cattle. Gigantic **combines** roar over the long grain fields where teams of horses once marched. Animals live in fancy barns filled with row upon row of steel pens until they are sent to market. The barnyard is often empty.

On many farms today you find only one kind of animal or crop. Farmers are often **specialists.** They raise only beef cattle for meat, or dairy cattle for milk. They keep only pigs, sheep, or horses. They specialize in growing wheat or corn. Some farmers are market gardeners. They grow only fruit and vegetables. There are a few farmers who make their livings growing Christmas trees!

Past and present

Look around you the next time you travel across the countryside. You will see that there have been many changes on the farms since the days of the settlers. Keep looking. You will probably see some beautiful old family farms. On these farms you can find clues to the history of this country. The story of farm life is a large part of the history of this country, and it is still an important part of our present.

Glossary

apiary a place for keeping bees

axle a bar on which a wheel or pair of wheels turns

barley a grass-like plant with grains that are used in breakfast cereals and other foods

blacksmith a person who makes things out of iron

brand a mark burned into the skin of cattle to show who owns them

buckwheat a plant with triangular seeds that are used to make flour

bull the adult male of cattle

bushwhack to make your way through woods by cutting at branches; the tool used to do this cutting

calcium a silvery substance, found in bones, shells, and milk, which is necessary for the growth of bones and teeth

caraway a plant with strongly flavored seeds that are sometimes baked in rye bread

carcass the body of a dead animal

card to brush wool fibers using a comb with metal or wire teeth in order to straighten the fibers before spinning

chaff the stiff, straw-like coverings of wheat, oats, rye, and other grains, separated from the seed by threshing

cion (sye-un) a twig from a tree used for grafting

combine (kom-bine) a machine that cuts, cleans, and threshes grain

conformation the way in which the parts of something are arranged

corn a tall cereal plant with grains that grow in rows on the large ears

cylinder a container in the shape of a tube with open ends

dairy the part of a barn where milk and cream are stored or made into butter and cheese

disk a flat, circular piece of metal

fennel a plant, related to parsley, with seeds that are used to flavor foods

fertilize to cause something to start growing

fertilizer manure or certain chemicals added to soil to make it richer

foal a young horse less than one year old

fork a large tool with a long handle and sharp prongs, used to lift hay, straw, and manure

furrow a long, deep groove made in the ground by a plow

grain the plant or the seeds of such cereal plants as wheat, oats, corn, and barley

granary the place where seeds of grain are stored

grindstone a flat stone disk that can be turned on an axle to sharpen tools

guinea hen a bird with dark gray feathers speckled with white

gutted having the insides of something removed

hay grass, clover, or other plants that have been cut and dried for use as animal food

heifer a young cow that has not yet given birth

hollyhock a tall garden plant with large flowers of various colors

hominy coarsely ground kernels of corn used as food when boiled in milk or water

husk the dry outer covering of certain seeds or fruits, such as an ear of corn

Indian corn any variety of corn; the word "Indian" was used by the settlers because in England "corn" could mean any kind of grain

irrigate to supply land with water through streams or pipes

kernel a seed of the corn plant or a grain of wheat or other cereal

kindling sticks or small pieces of wood used to start a fire

lard the melted fat of pigs

lasso a long rope that has a loop with a slipknot at one end; it is used for catching cattle and horses

livestock farm animals such as cattle, horses, sheep, and pigs

lovage a plant, related to parsley, with seeds that are used to flavor foods and homemade medicines

lye a strong solution made by straining water through ashes, used in making soap

mill the building where grain is ground into flour

miller the person who operates a mill

mow the place in the barn where hay and straw are stored

mower a machine that cuts grass or grain

mortar a thick bowl in which materials are crushed with a pestle

nectar a sweet liquid found in flowers and collected by bees to make honey

notch to cut a mark in a tree

oats a grass-like plant with seeds that are used as food by people and as feed for livestock

organic coming from living things; decaying leaves are organic materials used to make soil rich

parsnip an herb with a large carrot-like root that is eaten as a vegetable

passenger pigeon a wild pigeon, once common in North America, that has been extinct since the late 1800s

pennyroyal a plant with a strongly scented oil that is used in homemade medicines

pestle a tool shaped like a club and used for crushing something in a mortar

pitch a black, sticky substance that comes from pine trees and other evergreens

produce (pro-doos) fruit, vegetables, and other products grown on the farm

quince a hard, yellow, sour fruit, similar to an apple

racking off removing the sediment from cider

rafter a sloping beam that helps form and support a roof

ram a male sheep

reaper a machine that cuts and gathers a crop

rosemary an evergreen shrub with leaves that are used to flavor foods

rue a small bush with bitter-tasting leaves that are used in homemade medicines

rye a cereal grass, similar to wheat, with grains that are used to make flour and as animal food

sage a plant, related to mint, whose gray-green leaves are used to flavor foods

sapling a young tree

savory a plant, related to mint, with narrow leaves that are used to flavor foods

sediment small pieces of matter that settle at the bottom of a liquid

seeder a machine that sows seeds

shanty a rough, quickly built shack or cabin

sheaf a bundle of cut grain

shear to cut the wool from a sheep

skein a length of wool wound in a long, loose coil

sow (rhymes with no) to spread or scatter seeds over the ground; to plant

sow (rhymes with now) a fully grown female pig

staple a basic food or other common item, such as flour and sugar

stook a collection of sheaves propped together

straw the dried stems of grains or other grass-like plants

teat the nipple on a cow's udder, through which milk is drawn

thyme a small plant, related to mint, with leaves that are used to flavor foods

tick a small blood-sucking insect

udder the organ of a cow, goat, or sheep from which milk comes

wheat a grass that has thin, hollow stems and long, thin leaves; its tiny grains are used to make flour and other foods

wormwood a strong-smelling, bitter-tasting herb

underbrush small trees and shrubs growing under trees

yoke a wooden frame used to join together two work animals

Index

Acknowledgements

Library of Congress, Dover Archives, Colonial Williamsburg, Century Village, Lang, Upper Canada Village, Black Creek Pioneer Village, Metropolitan Toronto Library, Colborne Lodge, Toronto Historical Board, Gibson House, City of Toronto Archives, Bibliotheque National du Quebec, Harper's Weekly, Canadian Illustrated News, Public Archives of Canada, Notman Photographic Archives, Little Wide Awake, Frank Leslie's Illustrated Magazine, the Osborne Collection of Early Children's Books, Toronto Public Library, the Buffalo and Erie County Public Library Rare Book Department, Jamestown, Chatterbox, McCord Museum, Harper's Round Table Magazine, John P. Robarts Library, Massey-Ferguson Limited.

123456789 BP Printed in Canada 09876543